# POEMS FROM THE

# FIRST VOYAGE

# POEMS FROM THE FIRST VOYAGE

## David Capps

*The Nasiona*
San Francisco

*POEMS FROM THE FIRST VOYAGE*

Copyright © David Capps 2019

Published by *The Nasiona*

All rights reserved. No reproduction, copy, or transmission, in whole or in part, may be made without written permission.

For information contact :

nasiona.mail@gmail.com

https://thenasiona.com/

Front cover image :

Back cover image:

ISBN: 978-1-950124-08-4

# Contents

INTRODUCTION .................................................................................... VII

PROLOGUE TO THE KING AND QUEEN OF SPAIN ............................. 1

THE SHAPE OF THE EARTH .................................................................. 3

SIGNS OF LAND ..................................................................................... 4

FIRST ENCOUNTER ................................................................................ 5

THINGS OF SMALL VALUE .................................................................... 6

INCLINATIONS ....................................................................................... 7

PINE GROVES ......................................................................................... 8

LOST IN TRANSLATION ......................................................................... 9

GIVING THANKS .................................................................................. 10

PLAYING DRESS-UP ............................................................................. 11

DEC. 25-26, 1492: THE WRECK OF THE SANTA MARIA .................. 12

SAILING FROM THE ISLAND OF SANTA MARIA DE LA CONCEPCION TO FERNANDINA ISLAND ........................................................................ 15

MANATEES ........................................................................................... 16

RIVERS .................................................................................................. 17

THE LAY OF THE LAND ....................................................................... 18

CANOES ................................................................................................ 19

*Poems from the First Voyage*

ALOE .................................................................................................. 20

A WHALE IS NOT A FISH ................................................................ 21

MATANINO, ISLE OF WOMEN ....................................................... 22

COLLATERAL DAMAGE .................................................................. 23

COLUMBUS DREAMS ...................................................................... 24

TEMPEST SUPERSCRIPTION ........................................................ 26

ABOUT THE AUTHOR ..................................................................... 29

David Capps

# INTRODUCTION

We often find ourselves fascinated by the figures of history and seeking to know more. Sometimes, we want to know more than it is reasonable to demand. Historical method has its limitations. What would it mean to uncover the truth about the psyche of any "great" (and I emphasize the quotes) figure of history, given the polarizing effect of historical method itself upon uncovering that truth, and the near-mythologized character of the figure as depicted in popular culture? We (students of history, philosophers, scholars, poets, etc.) can ask this question of Jesus, Confucius, Socrates; in general, we might ask it of any lives and personalities that tend to elude well-rounded biographical treatment and the category of historical accuracy. In this work I ask it of Christopher Columbus.

How do I mean "true" or "accurate"? Poetry understands these cognates in relation to a *naming*, an awareness which, paradoxically, sees through the referential opacity of its own medium. Poets, whatever their pretensions, have not abandoned the supposition that naming delivers an essence. Historians see truth or accuracy as convergence, an approximation based on a variety of salient sources and types of evidence—ships' logs, documents, interpretations of ruins, etc. Yet, when history alternatively praises and demonizes a subject, when there is a holiday named after a figure that is simultaneously decried, when there is scant evidence available about the figure, perhaps poetic craft can serve as an alternative methodology.

What I have in mind with this work is history *as* poetry, not poetry *as* (alternative) history; it is not a re-writing, or a whitewashing of pre-existing historical facts. It is an experiment. It is an experiment not concerned with *events* at all, but with finding that place that existed before the fall of the "New World," as it were—before slavery, before colonization, before exploitation, before atrocities committed in the name of religion—in short, before everything that is normally conjured up by the word "Columbus"—because before all of this, there was a *guy* who was (as you will see) extremely *odd*—you might say that the banality of his evil consisted in a *surfeit* rather than deficit of imagination—who set out on a voyage so unfamiliar that there was *bound* to be some poetry implicit in his floundering attempts to describe what he saw.

Yeah, he was really fucking weird. I'm a poet and I couldn't help but be interested in whether this supreme bullshitter to the Queen of Spain—far from his only target—had, in spite of himself, certain descriptions that derived, in spite of his aims, from the confrontation with a land unfamiliar, and were poetic in quality. A person can be weird yet not inconsistent; I will say (no spoilers) that Columbus does have a peculiar tendency toward self-undermining, which is intensified by the concision of poetry. To say any more would be a spoiler.

A note on my methodology: poetry based on incorporating the source documents of others, sometimes with little or no alteration, but with sensitivity to the new context in which they are placed, we might call appropriation-based poetry.[1] This work is an example. It has a long history—extending perhaps as far back as poetry itself, insofar as poets have always been apprised of slang, phraseology particular to place and time, the occasional metaphor snatched away from a context of ordinary speech. Modernist poets like Ezra Pound, Robert Hayden, and William Carlos Williams were among some of the most vocal advocates of appropriation-based poetry in the 20th century, and were well aware of its benefits in regards to Pound's maxim to "make it new."

Among these poets there was a lot of variety in the kinds of texts they were drawn to appropriate, and importantly, the reasons they were appropriated. For example, Pound sometimes incorporated Chinese characters into his work because he felt it provided a better medium than English in order to cut through to the underlying image, while Hayden in his work "Middle Passage" incorporated historical documents pertaining to slave trade as a way of giving the reader a more comprehensive view of perspectives on slave trade.

---

[1] It is worth noting that the word "appropriation" also circulates as an expression in social theory, referring to the (usually piecemeal) appropriation of identities of marginalized cultural groups; yet works in this genre can also be seen as commenting on how the appropriators themselves (who belong to the dominant group) can have their identities appropriated, i.e., whose status as "great" needs to be thrown into question, either because of the connection to the appropriation of cultural identity through colonization, or inflated historical significance to which appropriation poetics can be a corrective, drawing attention *away from* their dubious grounds for celebration.

The document that I drew upon in constructing the work is the *Diario* of the first voyage, originally written by Columbus and then later transcribed by the Spanish monk, Bartolomé de las Casas. I utilized exclusively phraseology—what did he attempt to name/describe—that occurs in this source-text (as opposed an attempt to fabricate an inner life for Columbus out of my own inevitable biases=fail/inauthentic) with the idea to reveal facets of Columbus's idiosyncratic and contradictory personality, to provide with the resources available to me, a portrait of "what it is like to be'" Columbus.[2]

So, on one hand, *Poems from the First Voyage* can be read as a historical experiment; on the other, it continues the tradition of the appropriation-based poetics of the modernists.

Finding this voice has been a very careful process of writing, and rewriting the text, preserving elements of its idiosyncrasies and spontaneous sense of the unknown, while abstracting away from the elements of the *Diario*, the mundane (often navigational and inventorial) details that would weigh it down, not to mention omnipresent hints to royalty of "here's what'll justify the next venture." But the Columbus I found (and this is will no doubt ricochet off of your conceptions of him, hopefully) is a voice of obsession verging at times upon paranoia, a voice of borderline narcissism complicated by apparent sympathy, of urgent wanderlust driven by a strong sense of Providence, devotion and legacy; and at times, a simple, homesick Andalusian sailor who does not know what to expect next.

David Capps

---

[2] Philosophically, the present work might be seen as an intra-species instance of Thomas Nagel's article 'What is it like to be a bat?' where I use the *Diario* in an attempt to imagine what it is like for Columbus to be Columbus, as opposed to imagining what it is like for myself to be Columbus.

David Capps

# PROLOGUE TO THE KING AND QUEEN OF SPAIN

And for you that you granted me
great favors and ennobled me that

I from then on might call myself
"Don" and would be Grand Admiral

of the Ocean Sea and Viceroy
and perpetual Governor

of all the islands and lands that I might
discover and gain and from now on

might be discovered and gained
in the Ocean Sea. And likewise

my eldest son would succeed me
and his son him from generation

and generation forever. And as part
of my duty I thought it well to write

an account of my voyage very
punctually, to describe each night

what passed in the day, and to note
each day how I navigated at night,

to put it all down in a picture,
as it were, a great labor, by latitude

*Poems from the First Voyage*

from the equator and western longitude.
That I might accomplish these labors

above all it is very important
that I forget sleep.

David Capps

# THE SHAPE OF THE EARTH

I have always read that the world
comprising land and water
was spherical, testified by Ptolemy
and others who have proved it:

by eclipses of the moon,
observations made east to west,
as well the elevation of the pole
from north to south.

But I have seen so much irregularity
respecting the earth, that it is of the form
of a pear, round except where the stalk grows,
at which part it is most prominent

or like a round ball, upon one part of which
is a prominence like a woman's nipple,
this protrusion being highest nearest
the sky, situated under the equinoctial line

and at the eastern extremity of this sea—
I call that where the land and islands end.

*Poems from the First Voyage*

# SIGNS OF LAND

Sea water that is less salty, smooth as a river.
A tropic bird, white, which does not sleep at sea.
Softer breezes, rolling signs
from God's west, God whose hands hold victory.

A dolphin, which the men of the *Nina* kill.
A crab, which I keep as we move forward.
Sweeter breezes, rolling signs
from God's west, God whose hands hold land.

A booby comes to the ship, then a tern, a dove,
a river bird in thick green weed.
But when the sea rose high with no wind, the men
looked to me astonished:

Such a sign had not occurred since Moses.

# FIRST ENCOUNTER

Some paint themselves with black,
some paint themselves with white,
and some of them with red, and some
with whatever they can find.
        (I saw some with marks of wounds
        on their bodies)
Some of them paint their faces,
and some of them the whole body,
and some of them only the eyes,
and some only the nose.
        (I believed, and still believe
        that people from adjacent islands
        come here to take them prisoners)
Their hair is coarse—almost
like the tail of a horse—and short.
All of them go round
naked as their mothers bore them.
        (They will make good servants
        and intelligent.)

*Poems from the First Voyage*

# THINGS OF SMALL VALUE

Some of them I gave red beads,
which they put on their chests,
and many other things

of small value in which they took
so much pleasure.

Later they came swimming
to the launches and brought us
parrots and cotton thread

in balls and javelins and many other
things, and they traded them to us

for other things, which we gave them,
such as small glass beads and bells,
and they gave everything

for anything that was given to them,
and other little things

it would be tiresome to write down.

# INCLINATIONS

I was attentive, and took
trouble to ascertain if

there was gold, a small piece
fastened in a hole some of them

had in their nose, by signs
I was able to ascertain that

to the south there was a king
who had great cups full, who

possessed a great quantity...
I tried to get them to go there,

but afterwards I saw that they
had no inclination. Longing

to possess our things, and not
having anything in return

to give, they take what they
can get, presently swim away.

*Poems from the First Voyage*

# PINE GROVES

When the ships' boys shouted they saw pine groves,
I looked up from shining stones, toward mountains,

where I saw from their height and straightness, like
spindles, thick and thin, the ships that could be made,

vast quantities of planking and masts for the greatest
ships of Spain. I saw oak and arbutus, a river to make

water-powered sawmills, because as many ships
as might be wanted could be made bringing out

equipment except for wood and pitch, of which
a great plenty could be made. It pleases Our Lord

always to show me one thing better than the other,
in lands and groves and plants and fruits and flowers

as in people. And when to him who sees it it is so
admirable, how much more so will it be to him who

hears about it, and no one will be able to believe it
if he does not see it.

David Capps

# LOST IN TRANSLATION

I do not know the language, and the people
of these lands do not understand me nor do I,

nor anyone else that I have with me, them.
Many times I understand one thing said by

these Indians that I bring for another,
its contrary. They say any prayer we tell them

to say, and make the sign of the cross.
As fine as any carpenter could make.

They are not idolaters, nor do they have
a false religion.

*Poems from the First Voyage*

# GIVING THANKS

So many came that they covered the land, giving
a thousand thanks.

Some of them ran this way, others that way, to bring
us bread made from *niames*

> *Niamas*, roots like large radishes—their sustenance,
> have a flavor just like chestnuts,
>
> and there is no one who would not believe, eating them,
> that they are not chestnuts

which they call *ajes* and which are very white
and good,

and they brought us water in gourds, clay jugs
of a form like those of Castile,

they kissed our hands and feet, felt us, to try to see
if we were, like themselves, of flesh and bone.

> Don't say to yourself that they gave liberally
> because what they gave was of little worth,
>
> those who gave gold pieces gave as freely
> as those who had a calabash of water.

It is easy to know when a thing is given
with a heart desirous of giving.

# PLAYING DRESS-UP

Five kinds had come, all subject
to one called Guacanagari, all crowns
displaying their high rank.

Your Highnesses would take pleasure in seeing
how he took the crown from his own head
and put it on mine,

how I took from my own neck a collar
of fine agates and handsome beads
that looked well in all its parts

and put it on the kind; and took the fine red cape
I had dressed in that day,
and dressed the king, and put on his finger

a large silver ring, and sent for some colored,
high-laced shoes
and had him shod with them.

*Poems from the First Voyage*

# DEC. 25-26, 1492: THE WRECK OF THE SANTA MARIA

I

Midnight, dead calm, the sea as in a bowl, the crew
saw me lie down to rest, and left the helm to that boy—

ships were not to be steered by boys, no difference
whether wind or calm. When the boy felt the rudder ground

and heard the noise of the sea he cried out, I jumped up
instantly, ordered master of the ship to rouse the crew,

launch the small boat, take an anchor and cast it at the stern—
When I saw my crew fleeing, and waters shallowing, my ship

broadside to the sea—I did the only thing I could, ordered
the mast cut, ship lightened as much as possible, to see

if she would come off. Nothing more could be done, as
the water continued to rise, her side fell over across the sea,

nearly calm. Her timbers opened, though she remained
in one piece. I could not save her.

II

The king wept when he heard of the disaster,
sent all his people from the village with canoes

to help us, displayed great haste and diligence,
personally assisted the unloading, along with his brothers,

guarded what was taken ashore, sent one of his relatives
to console me, that I would not be troubled or annoyed,

for the king would give me whatever he possessed.
I certify to Your Highnesses that in no part of the Castile

could things be so secure—not even a shoe string was lost!
I certify to your Highnesses that in all the world I do not believe

there is a better people or a better country. They love
their neighbors as themselves,

and they have the softest and gentlest voices in the world
and are always smiling.

III

The king understood that I desired a great deal
of gold. He told me all about this gold, specifically,

that it is found in Japan. They brought me a large mask,
which had large pieces of gold

in the ears and eyes, and in other places,
which the king himself presented to me—by his manner

of eating, his decent behavior, and his exceptional
cleanliness, he showed himself to be of good birth—placed this,

along with other jewels of gold, on my head
and around me neck. I derived a great deal of pleasure,

consolation from these things, and when I realized
that this mitigated the affliction I experienced, I recognized

that Our Lord had caused me to run aground, that I might
establish a settlement here. I ordered that a lombard

and musket be fired. The king was spellbound
when he saw the effect of their force and what they penetrated.

When the people heard the shots, they fell to their knees.

IV

All of this was the will of God: the ship's running aground
so easily that it could not be felt, with neither wind nor wave;

the cowardice of the ship's master and some of the crew
(who were mostly from his part of Spain), who refused

my order to cast the stern anchor to draw the ship off;
the discovery of this country. The men remaining have timbers

with which to construct the fortress, provisions of bread
and wine for more than a year, as well as seeds for sowing,

and the ship's boat. I am leaving a caulker, a carpenter, a gunner,
and a caskmaker among the many men who desire zealously

to serve Your Highnesses, and who will please me greatly
if they find the mine where the gold comes from.

Everything that has happened was for this purpose,
that this beginning may be made.

David Capps

# SAILING FROM THE ISLAND OF SANTA MARIA DE LA CONCEPCION TO FERNANDINA ISLAND

I sailed.
I navigated.
I stood off and on all night.
I came.
I anchored.
I ordered.
I also ordered.
I sent the ships' boat for water (and the natives
with good will showed my people, brought full casks).
I have determined to sail around it, so far as
I can understand
there is a mine in it or near it.

Now, as
I am writing this
I made sail round the island, to navigate until
I find Samaot, an island or a city where there is gold
Say all the natives who are on board
And those of San Salvador, Santa Maria.
I saw no beasts on the island.
I have no doubt.

A boy told me that he saw a large serpent.

*Poems from the First Voyage*

# MANATEES

I saw three sirens
come up high out of the sea

they have a face like a man
in some ways

they are not as beautiful
as they are painted.

# **RIVERS**

At the foot of that Cabo de Campana,
an admirable harbor and a big river;
and a quarter of a league away, another

river; and from there a half league, another
river; and beyond, at another half league, another
river; and beyond, a league further, another
river; and another league beyond that, another
river; and after another quarter league, another
river; and another league beyond that, another big
river—coming thus along the coast, a great

settlement to the southeast of the last
river, men coming to the seashore shouting,
all naked, javelins in their hands.

I hauled down the sails, and anchored.

*Poems from the First Voyage*

# THE LAY OF THE LAND

As soon as dawn broke many of these people
came to the beach, all youths, a handsome people.
Their hair, loose and coarse, forehead broad,
more so than in any other people.

They have no iron, their darts being wands
without iron, some having a fish's tooth at the end,
others being pointed in various ways.
They neither carry nor know anything

of arms—for I showed them swords
and they took them by the blade
and cut themselves through ignorance.
This island is large and flat, and the people docile.

# CANOES

They came in small canoes to the ship, all of one piece,
made out of the trunk of a tree, like a long boat,
wonderfully, wonderfully worked,

some holding 45 men, some only large enough for one,
propelled with a paddle like a baker's shovel, and go at a marvelous,
marvelous rate.

If the canoe capsizes, they all promptly begin to swim, swim, to bale it out
with calabashes they take with them.

I observed that they quickly took in, quickly took in what was said.

*Poems from the First Voyage*

# ALOE

I see a thousand kinds of trees
each of which has its own kind
of fruit,
and they are as green now
as in Spain in May and June.

There are
a thousand kinds of plants, and the same
with flowers, and of everything, nothing
recognized

except this aloe.

It is
raining a lot without being
cold, rather the day is hot
and the nights temperate, as in May in Spain
in Andalusia.

There are no nightingales.

This is not like the rivers
of Guinea, which are all
pestilential.

David Capps

# A WHALE IS NOT A FISH

Here the fish are so unlike ours

that it is wonderful.

Some are the shape of dories, finest colors

in the world, blue, yellow, red, and other tints,

all painted in various ways, colors are so bright

that there is not a man who would not delight

in them, as at my ships' sails: mainsail and two

bonnets, foresail, spritsail, mizzen, and main top

sail; and the ship's boat at the stern.

Also there are whales.

*Poems from the First Voyage*

# MATANINO, ISLE OF WOMEN

Intercourse at Carib would be
difficult, as the natives are said
to eat human flesh, have only
one eye, and dogs' faces—still,

I determined to go there, and thence
to Matanino, as it was en route,
said to be populated by women,
without men. If males are born,

they are sent to the island of males,
if females, they remain with their
mothers. I could not understand
what else was said except by guessing.

# COLLATERAL DAMAGE

A dolphin, which men of the *Nina* kill.

A serpent, which we killed (and I am bringing
the skin to Your Highness).

Another serpent, seven palmos long.

A fish that looks just like a pig, not a porpoise,
all hard shell and nothing soft

except the tail and eyes

and a hole underneath for expelling its superfluities,
which I ordered salted to take to Spain.

A turtle the sailors killed,
its shell in the launch in pieces,

ships' boys gave the Indians pieces of it
the size of a fingernail, in return for javelins.

\*\*\*

Of the six youths I took captive
at the *Rio de Mares*

and ordered to go in the caravel *Nina*,
the two eldest fled.

*Poems from the First Voyage*

# COLUMBUS DREAMS

A light like a wax candle     six pounds in weight    rising
   and falling   in the distance    we shortened sail
and lay by    under the main sail     rising and falling
   like a wax candle   a light   in the distance   I made

land   be more distant   as we lay by   under the main sail
   without the bonnets    rising and falling     like a light
they could be more     easily converted    by love
   than by force   those who are more   subtle

women   wore a small piece of cotton    scarcely covered
   a light     a love   more easily converted    than by force
a wax candle   rising    and falling at intervals
   Indians raise   their hands   to the heavens      But I

see one who came from the ship    his face change color
     turned yellow as wax   trembling much   showing him
my crossbow    wax candle    rising and falling    a light

   let it be understood that they all     would be slain

my sword     unsheathed
    though he was a tall
       strong man
          turned yellow as wax
    trembling as they all fled
let them know
    that they would all be slain    more easily

converted
   by love than by force
       those subtle ones    the women

who wore a small piece of cotton        scarcely covered
                did not want to leave
the river
                but pulled towards the place

                where all had assembled
        painted in great numbers

                some with tufts of feathers on their heads

and all had their bundles of darts.

*Poems from the First Voyage*

# TEMPEST SUPERSCRIPTION

All believed it some act of devotion
when I threw the barrel, stoutly hooped,

into the sea, my writing in the cask
folded and sealed, wrapped in wax,

put into a kind of tart or cake of wax,
writing I directed to your Highnesses

with the superscription or promise
of a thousand ducats to him who should

deliver it unopened. I am aware that
I am in debt to the Most High Creator

for my life—what caused me boundless
grief was that, just now, the Divine Majesty

should will to block with my death the glory
I lent your Highnesses, the enlargement

of your high estate, and above all my grief
redoubled at the vision of my sons without succor

in a strange land, without my having rendered
(at least, without its being made manifest)

the service for which one might trust
your Highnesses to remember them.

Approaching Castile I made another package
just like that and placed it on the upper part

of the poop. If the ship should sink the barrel
might float at the will of fate.

# ABOUT THE AUTHOR

**DAVID CAPPS** received his PhD in philosophy from University of Connecticut and an MFA in poetry from Southern Connecticut State University. He is the author of *Love Through Literature: An Introduction to the Philosophy of Love and Friendship* (Kendall Hunt Press: 2019) and *A Non-Grecian Non-Urn* (Yavanika Press, 2019), an e-chapbook of poems based on his travels throughout Greece.

www.ingramcontent.com/pod-product-compliance
Lightning Source LLC
Chambersburg PA
CBHW060226050426
42446CB00013B/3187